Haiku for the Soul

Sue Stein

2017
Dragonstone Press
Rosemount, Minnesota

ISBN 978-0-9991801-1-2

Dragonstone Press
3820 120th St. W.
Rosemount, MN 55068

Dedicated to the beauty
and wonder of the land
and all its creatures

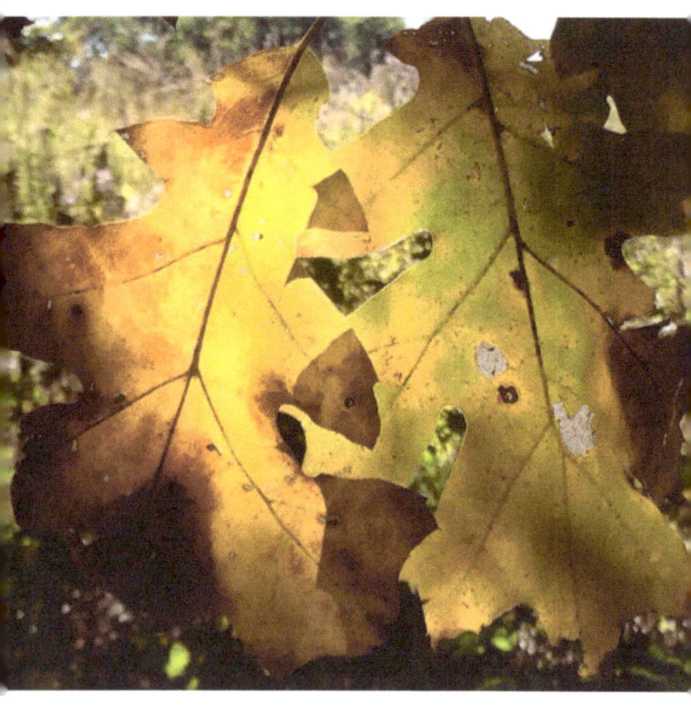

spotlighted by sun

two oak leaves are enjoying

their final hurrah

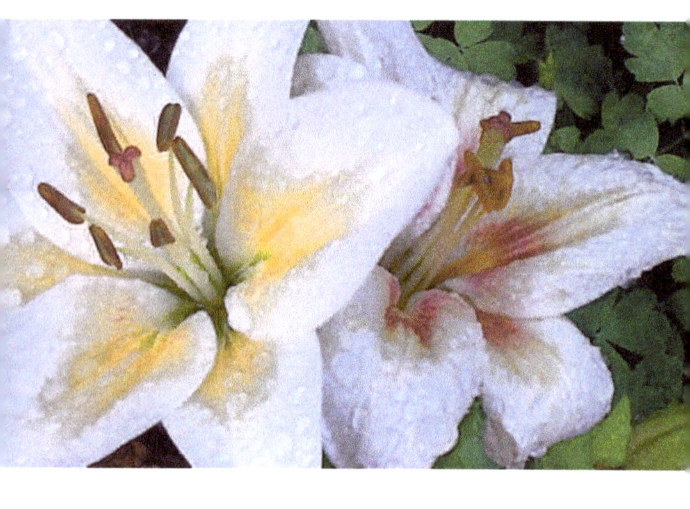

rain-speckled petals
softly spattering downward
the earth drinking deep

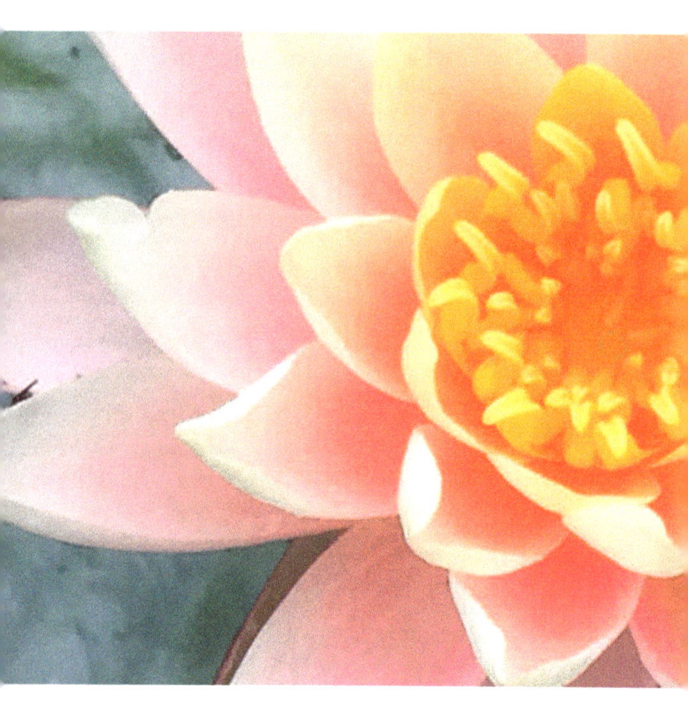

tropical lily

geometric precision

floral perfection

hidden behind mist

landscape struggles to emerge

a good day to sleep

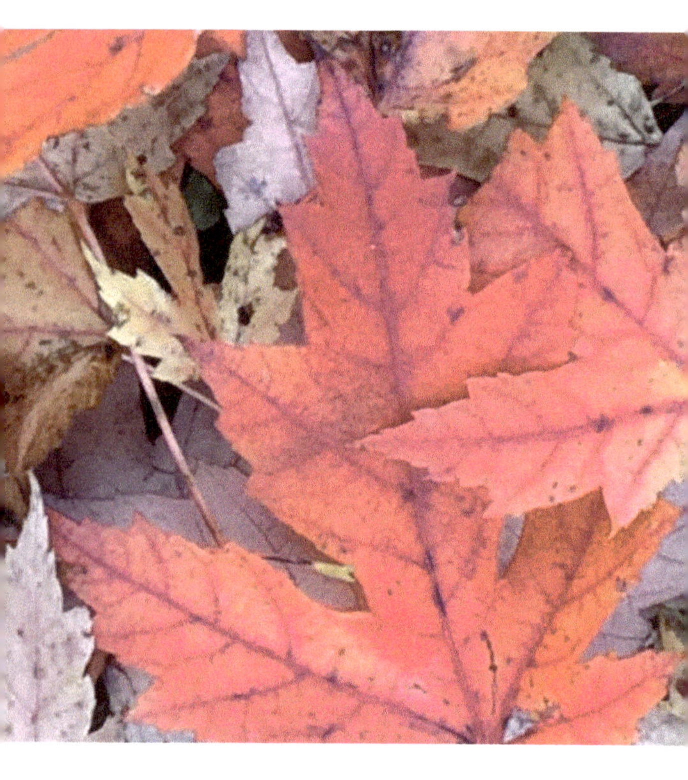

leaves blanket the ground

interplay of bright colors

tangy scent of dirt

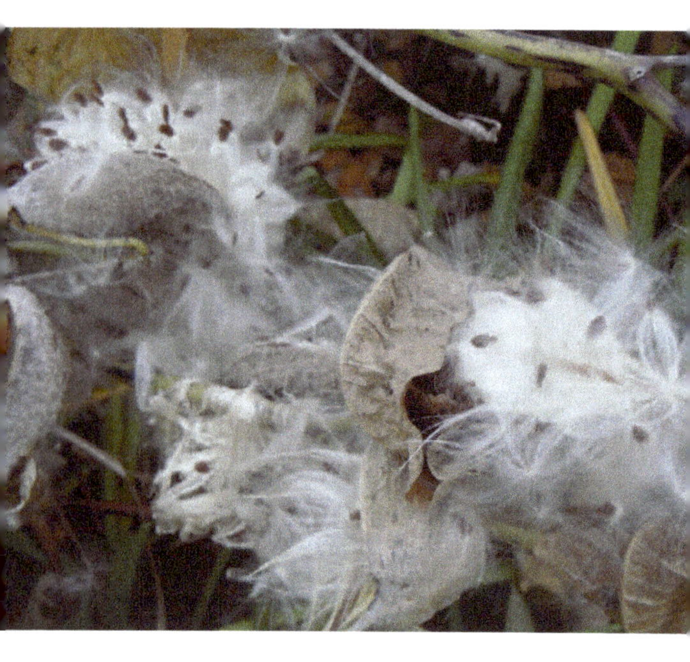

cotton candy puffs
eldritch filaments of white
bursting at the seams

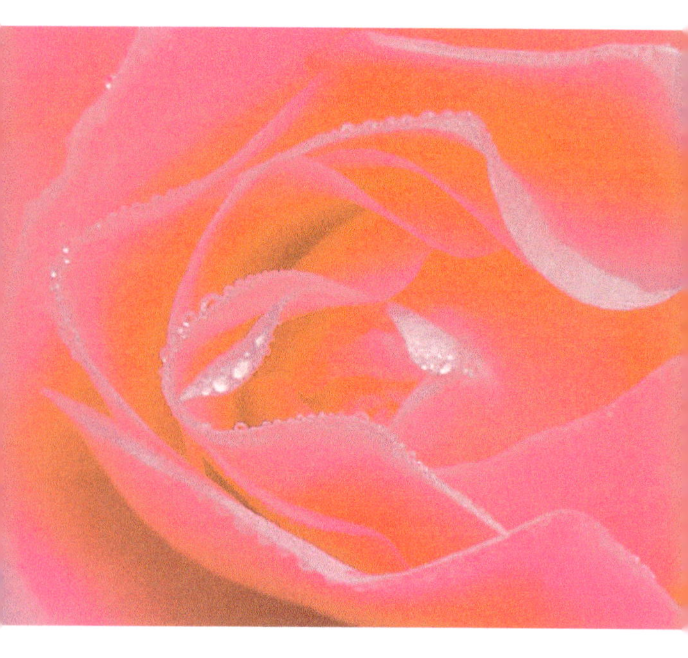

rosebud blossoming

water droplets trace the swirls

a ballet in pink

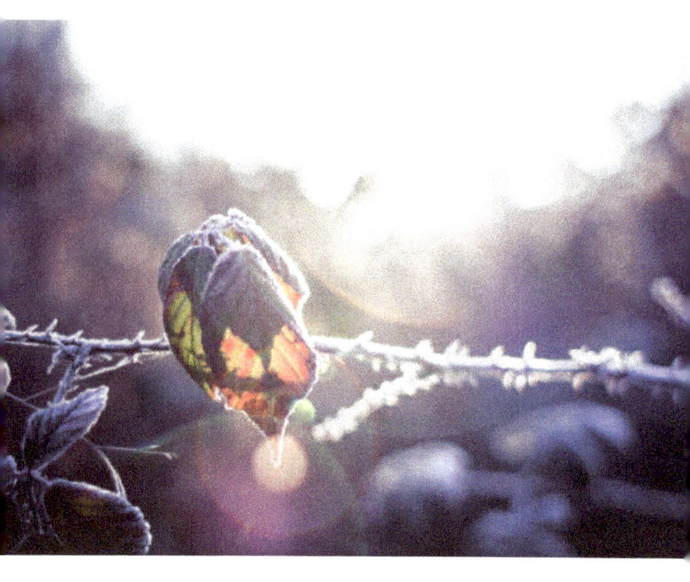

rime ice coating leaves

autumn colors fade away

hummingbirds long gone

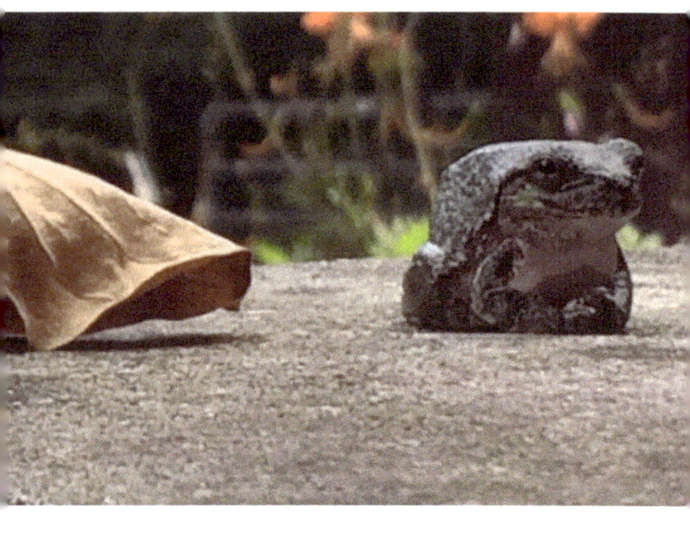

zen frog meditates

what is the meaning of life?

motionless he waits

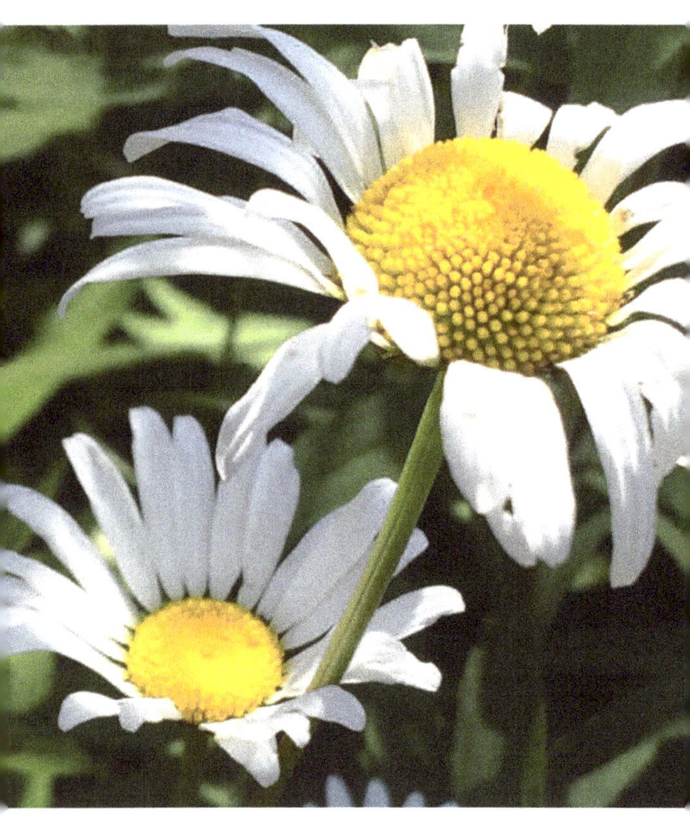

sunlight reflecting

pristine white and richest gold

a study in grace

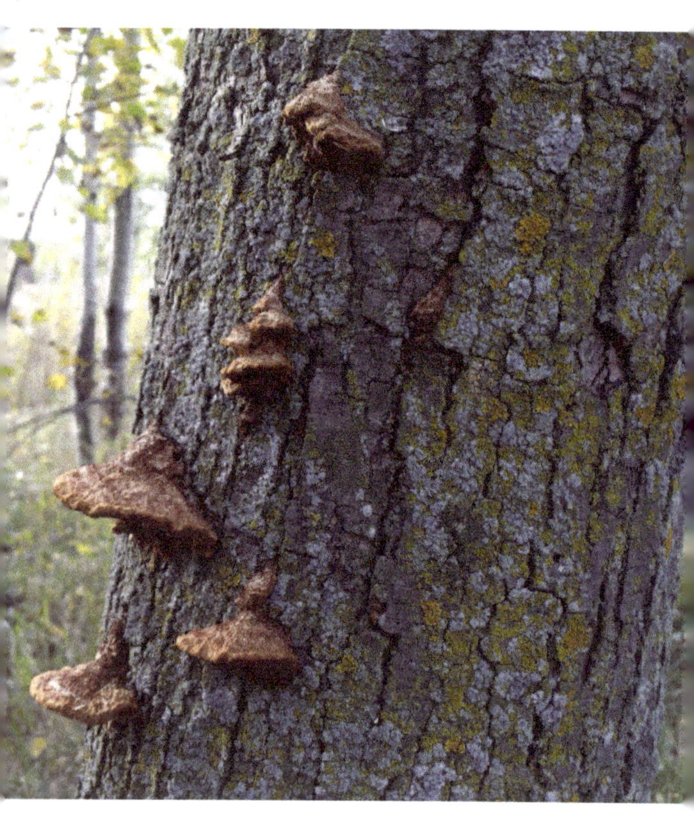

mushrooms climbing high

scaling an ancient oak tree

reaching for heaven

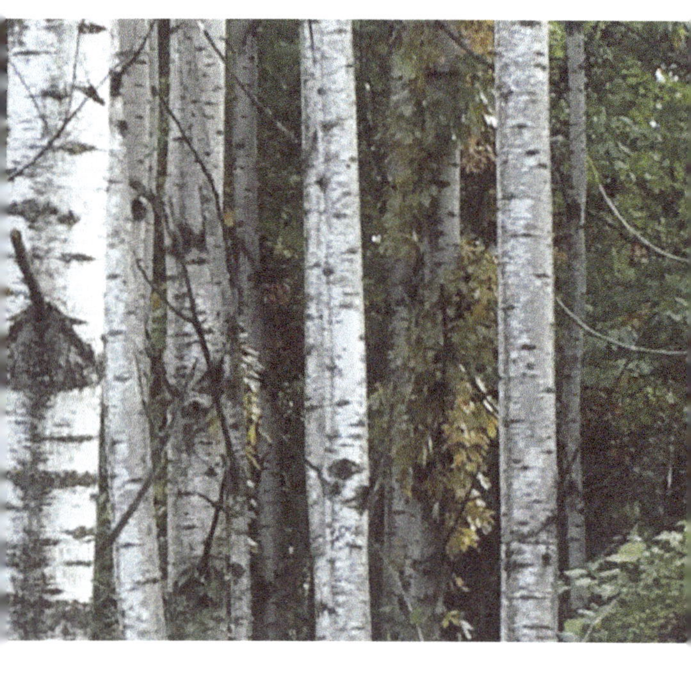

poplar leaves tremble

in the wind

a storm sweeping near

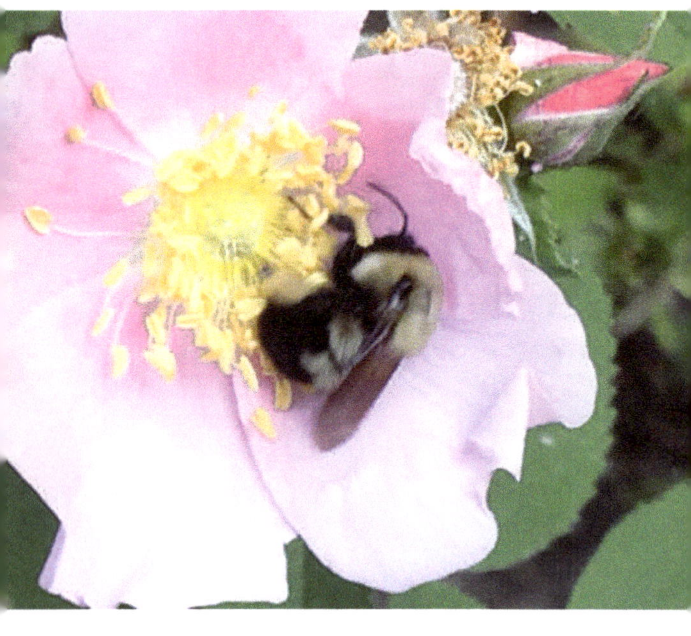

dancing bumblebee

harvesting the sweet nectar

savoring each drop

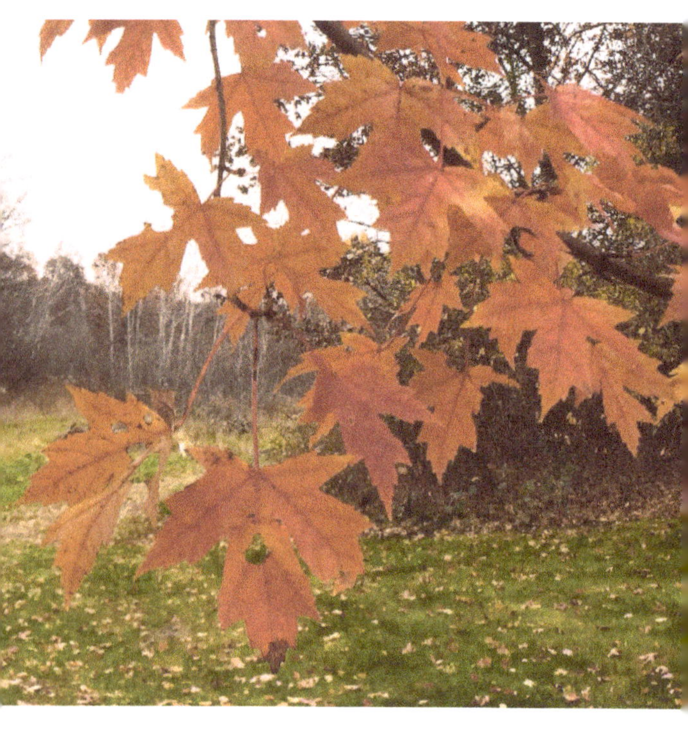

splashes of color

brightening a cloudy day

ruby red jewels

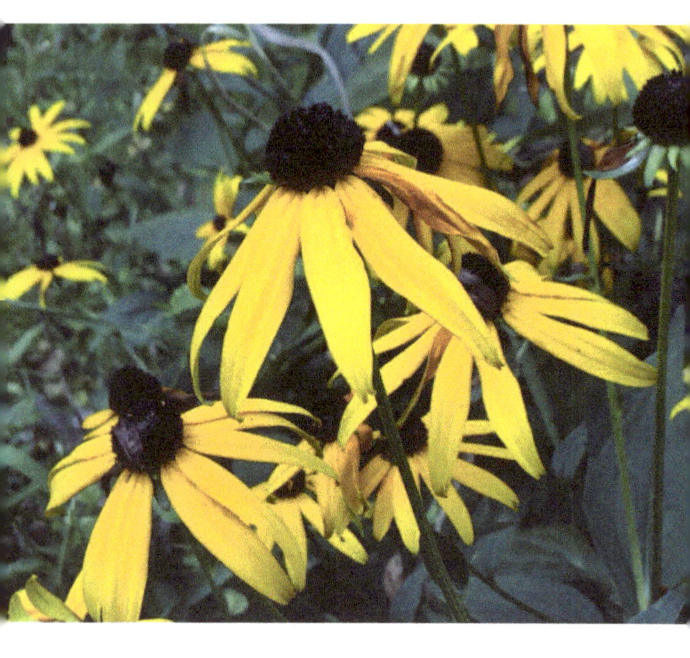

gold-colored petals

delicately drape to earth

a hug from the sun

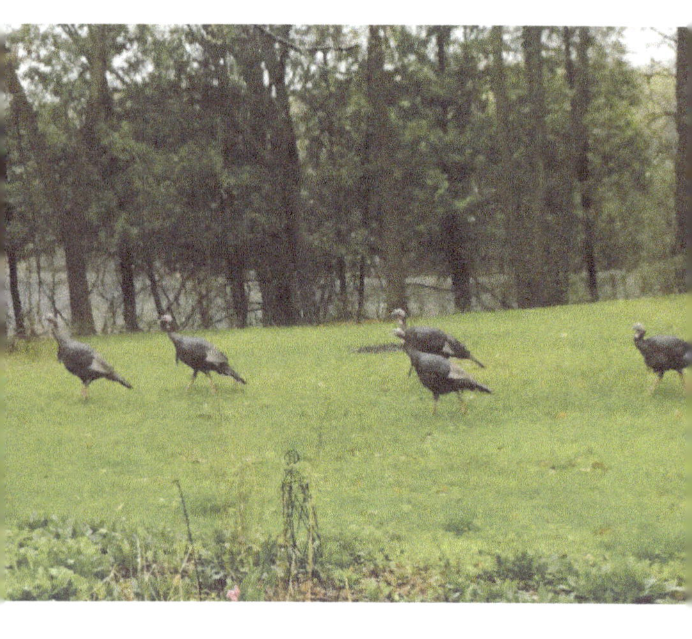

turkeys on parade
lining up in formation
across my backyard

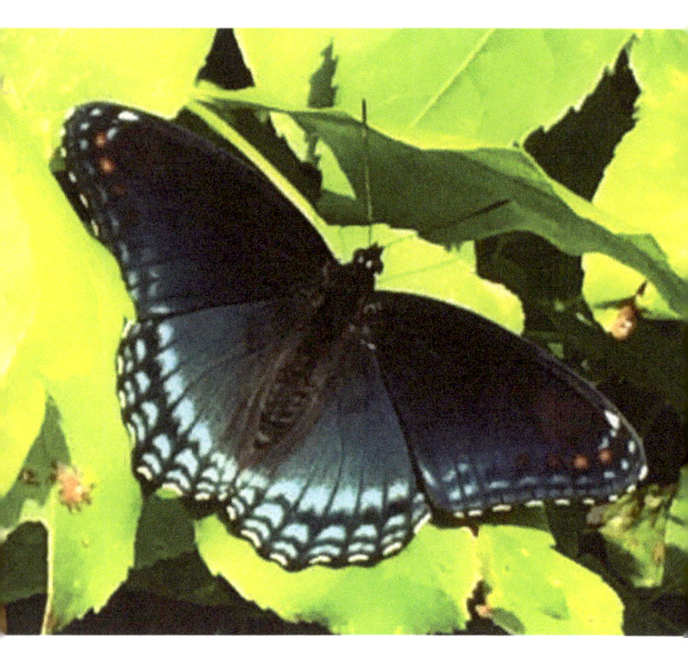

diaphanous wings

shimmer in reflected sun

coruscating light

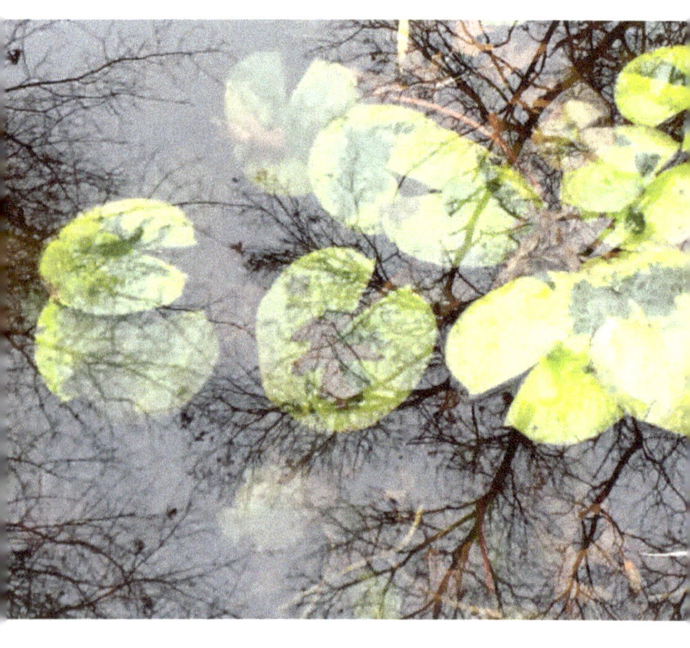

circlets of lime green

lily pads cover the pond

ready to emerge

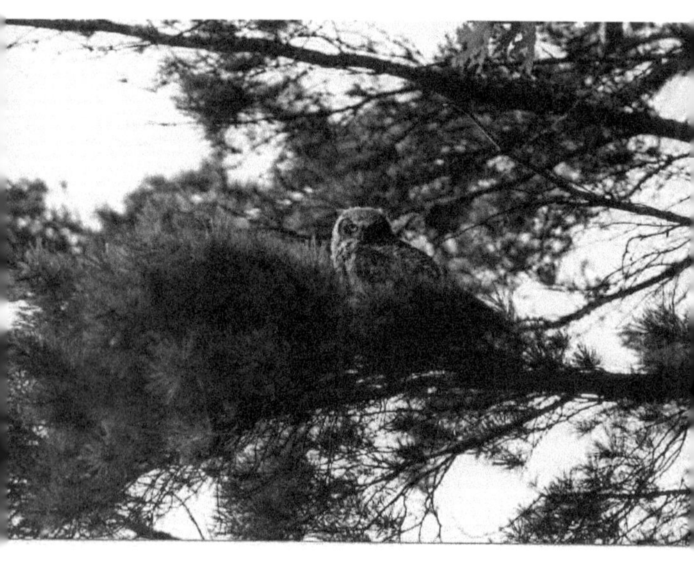

owl perching on limb
rabbit scurries for cover
the swooping of wings

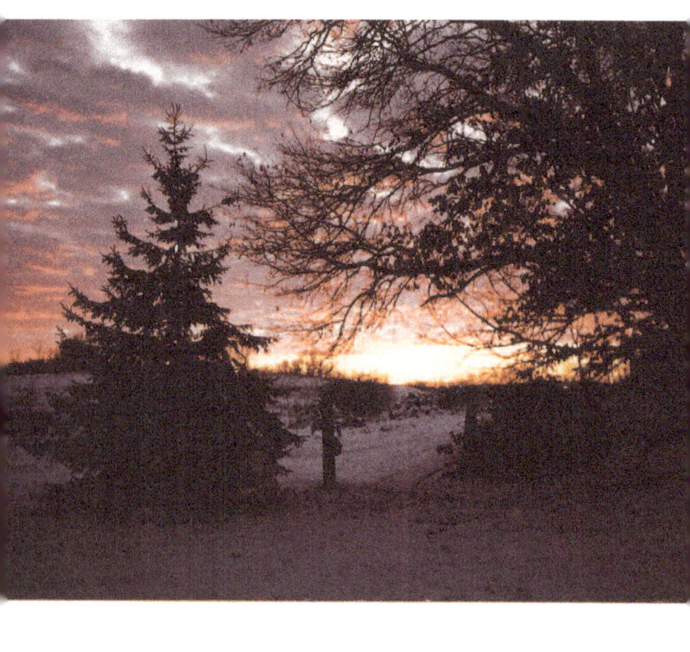

winter-bare branches

snow covering fallen leaves

a long wait for spring

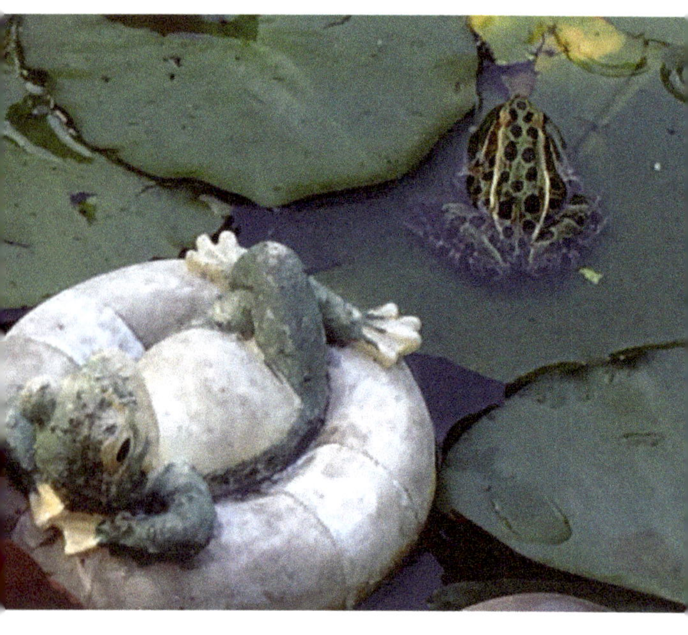

harbinger of spring

deafening bull frog chorus

fills the evening air

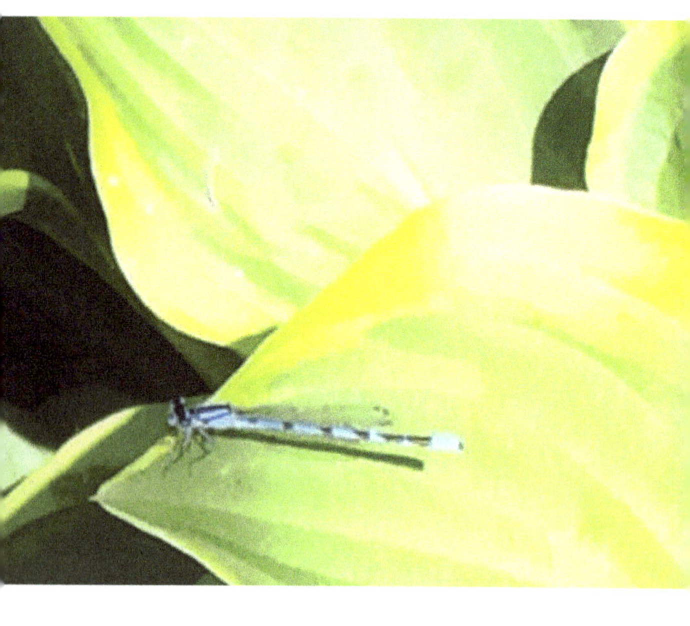

iridescent damselfly

a bright burst of blue

wings its way into my hear

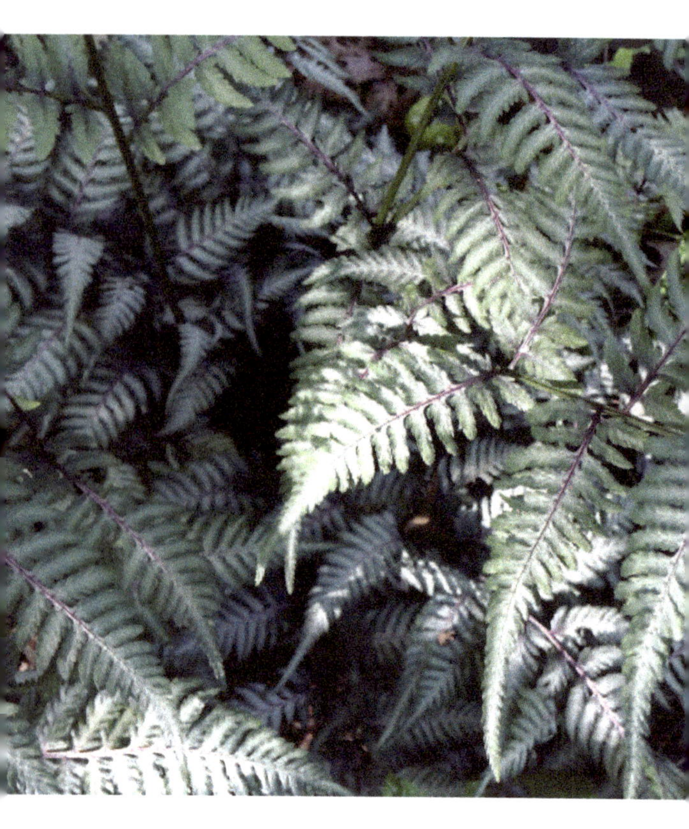

shifting dark and light

shadows dancing in the deep

what lies hidden there?

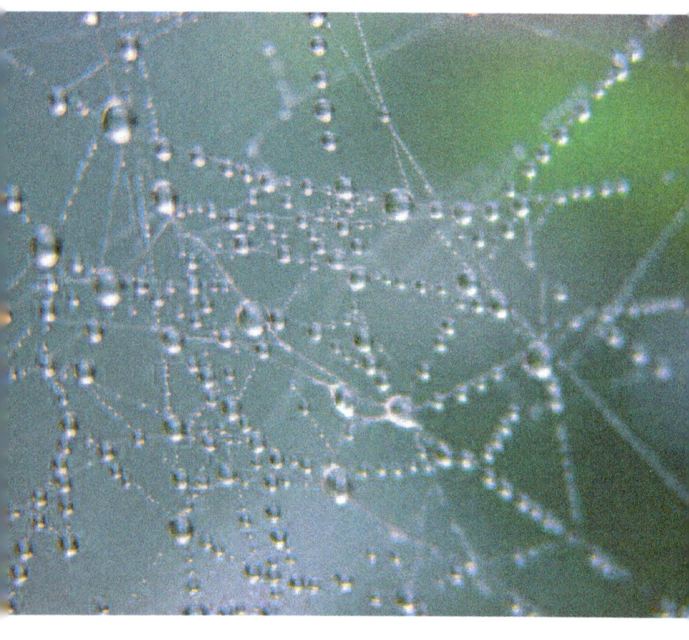

softly draping web

drifting on gossamer threads

ephemeral life

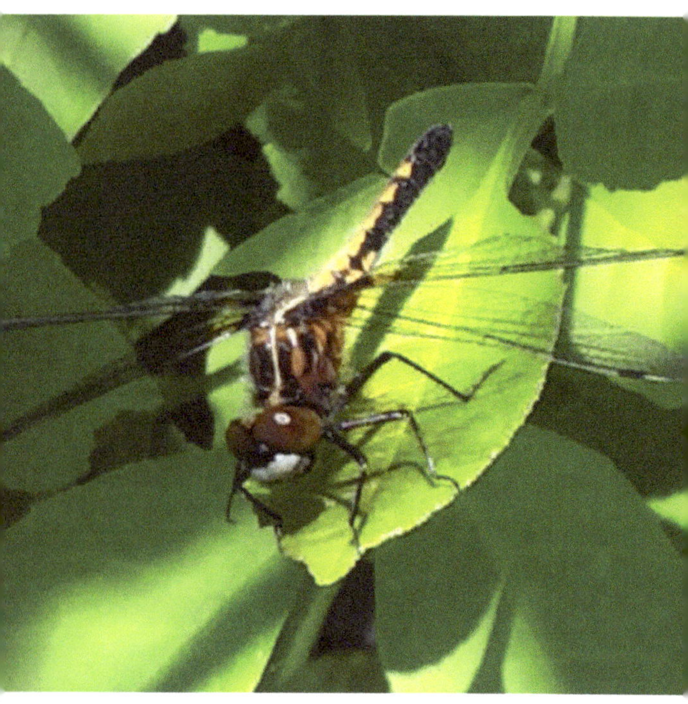

dragonfly soars near

multifaceted eyes gaze

deep into my soul

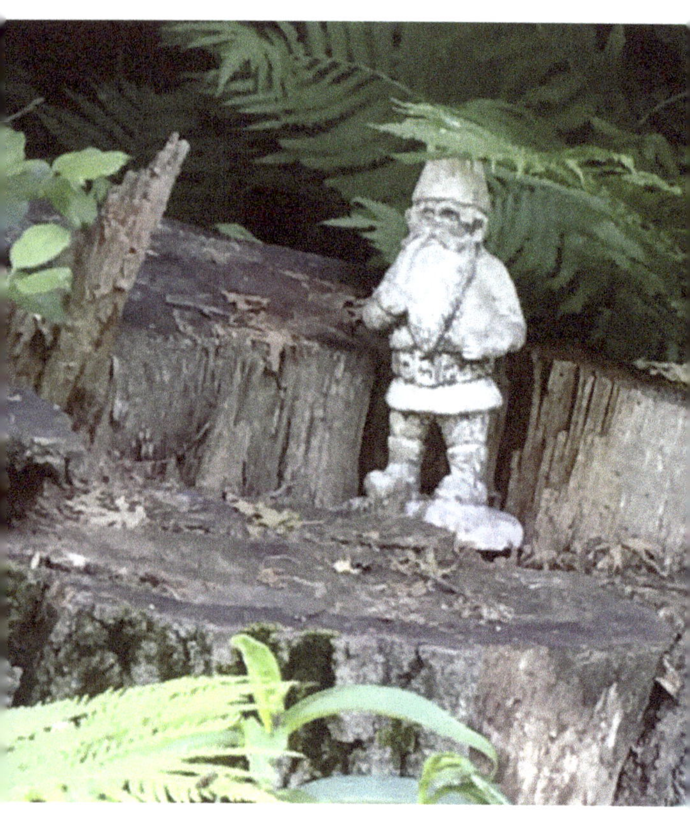

ancient sentinel

standing watch over the land

keeper of secrets

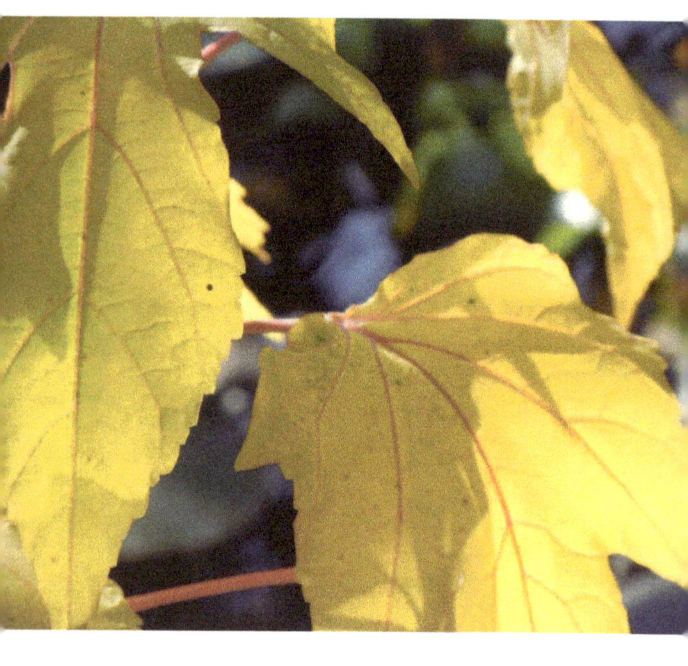

filtered sunlight gleams

arabesques of dancing leaves

soft breeze caresses

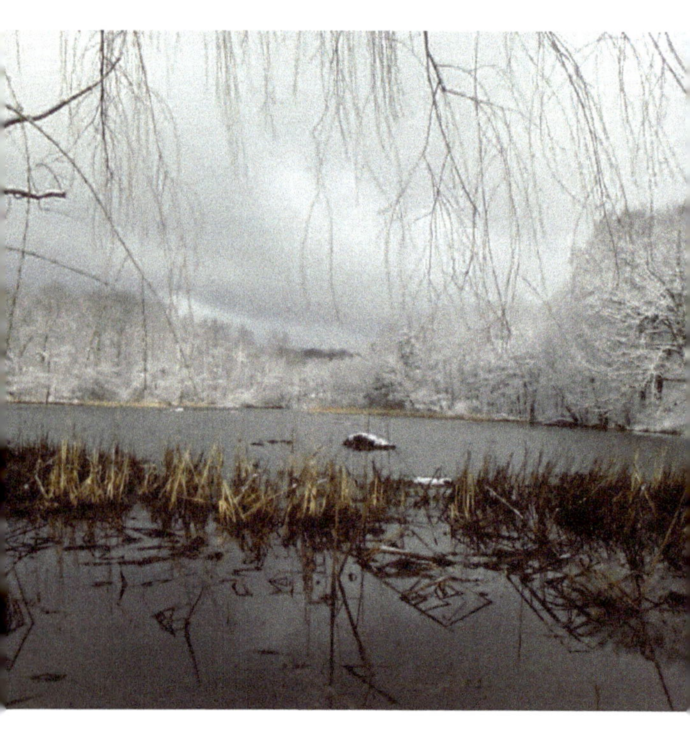

how sweet is winter

fresh snowfall blanketing trees

frosting on a cake

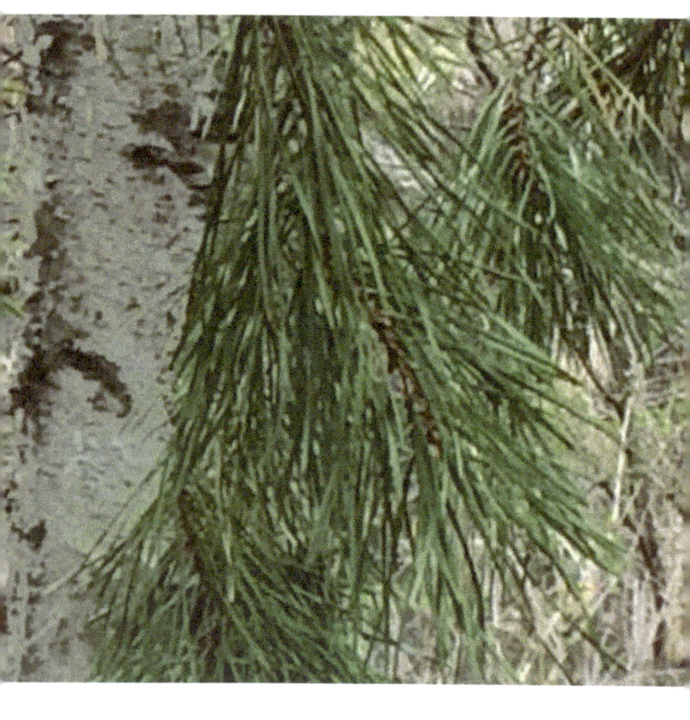

swaying in the breeze

pine boughs are

softly murmuring

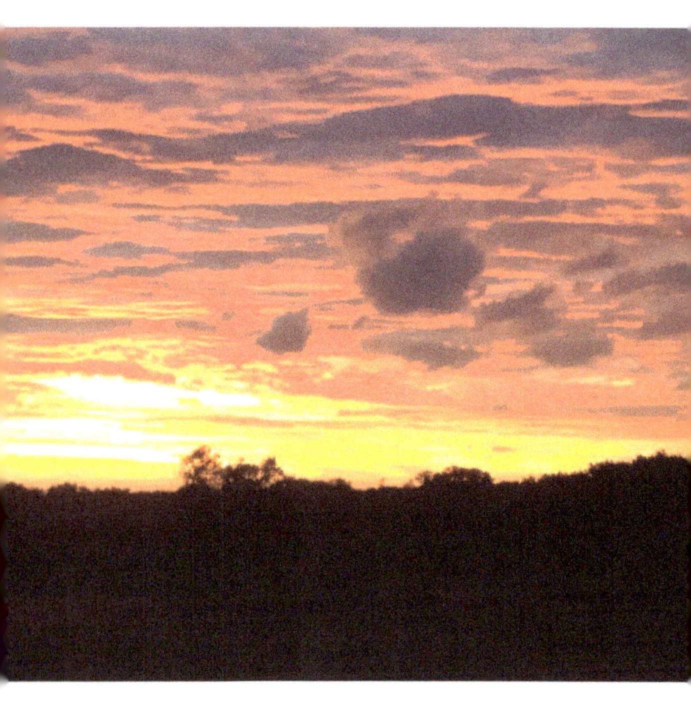

clouds race across sky

shadows fall

pale ships passing by

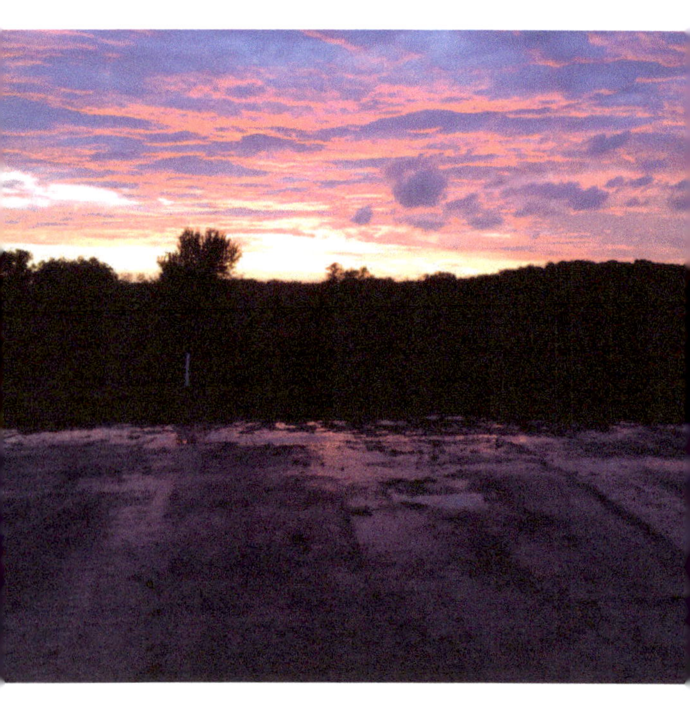

puddles of snowmelt

reflect the sky

as if it were earth

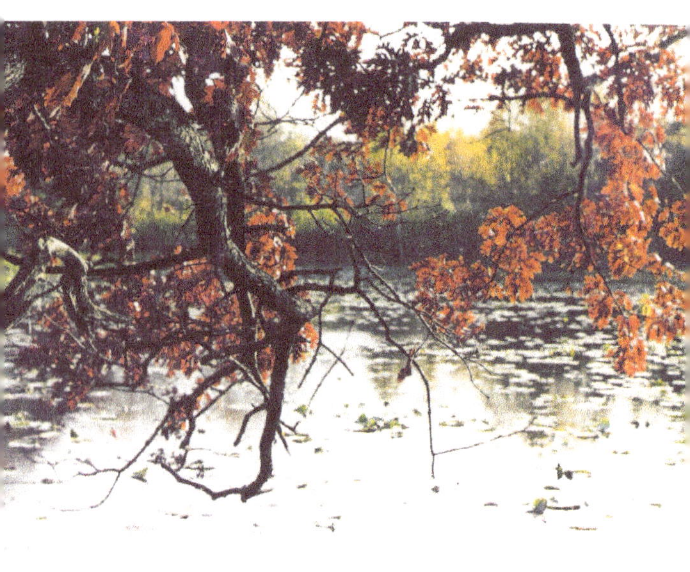

shadows flickering
through the trees
afternoon sunlight

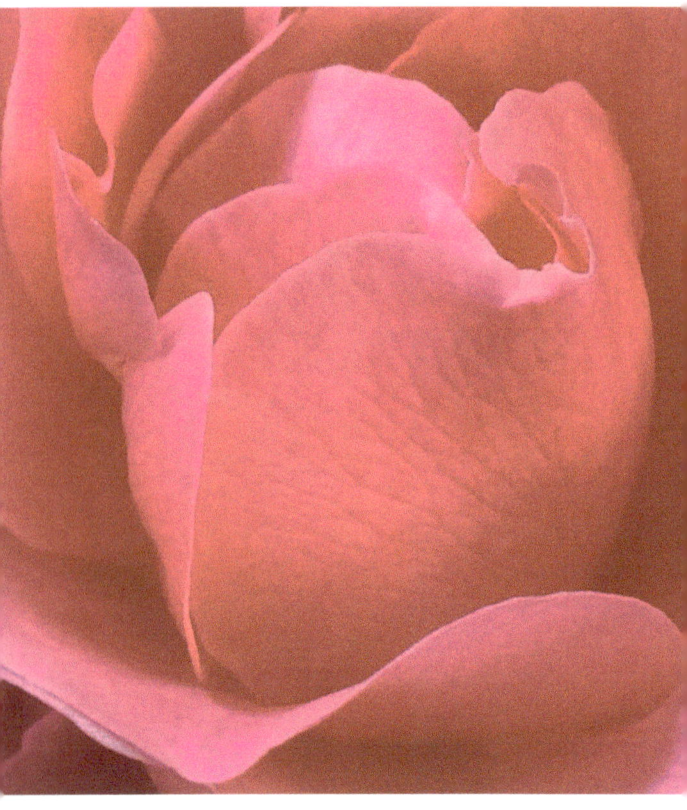

unfurling velvet

softly, slowly opening

pink burst of delight

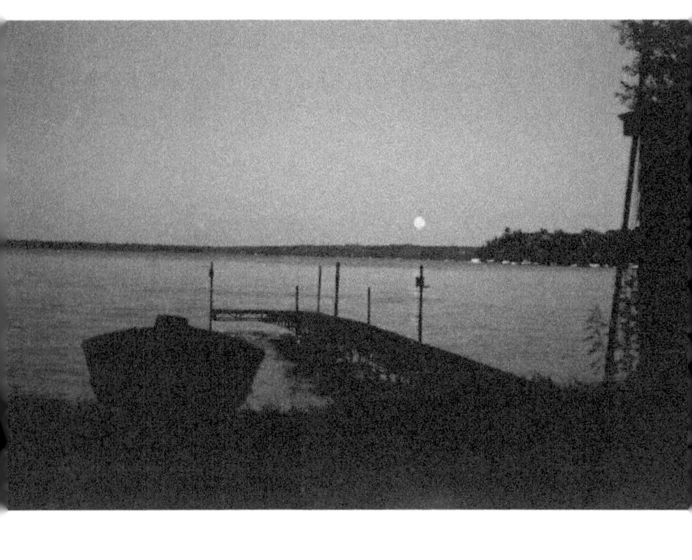

walk along the shore

loons calling out plaintively

moonbeams slice the night

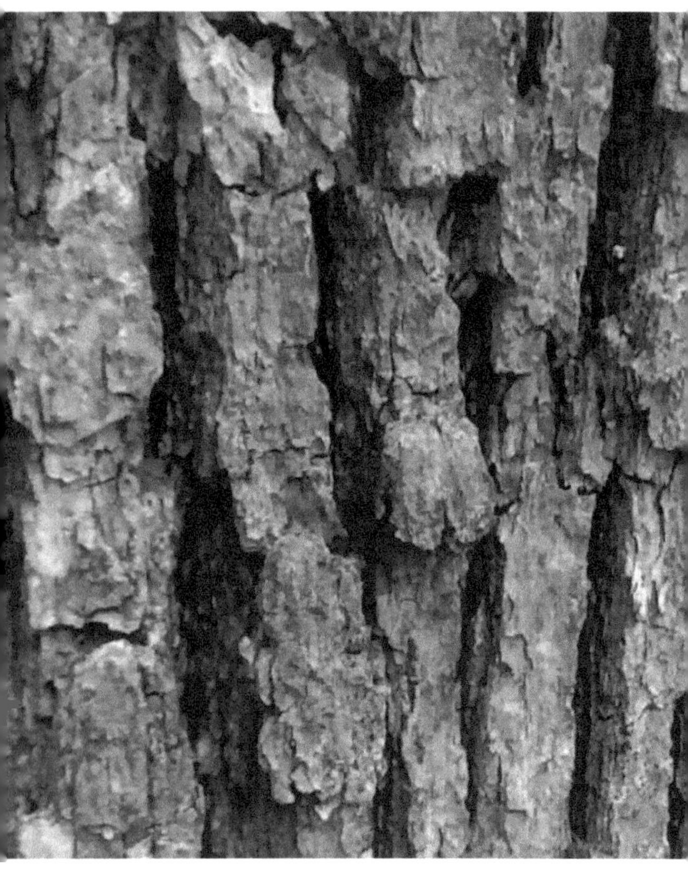

woodpecker drumming

oak tree sighs

no sleep for me now

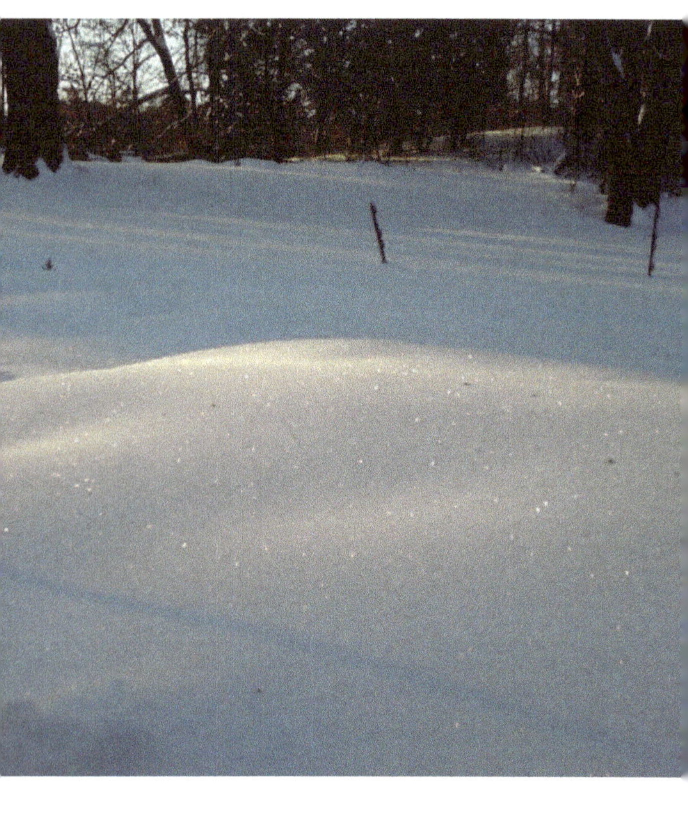

slanting blue shadows

diamond-scattered soft blanket

white meringue dessert

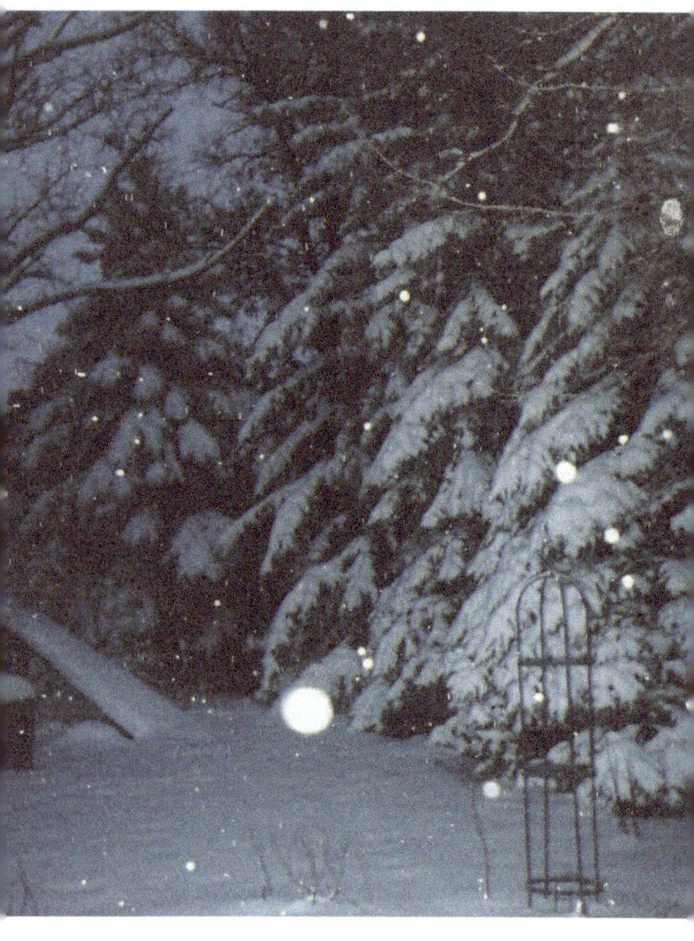

moonless snow-filled night

fairy orbs light up the trees

deep in the winter

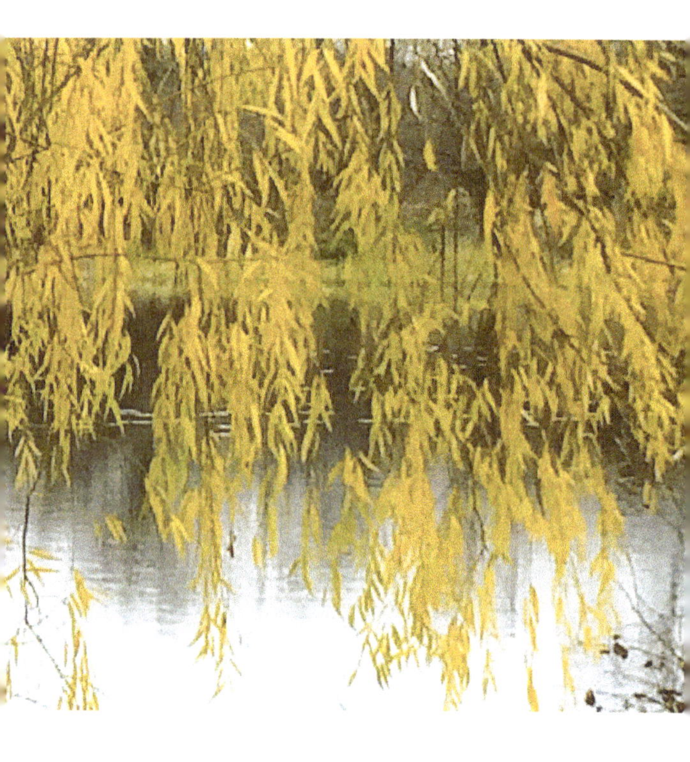

draping yellow fronds

willow leaves softly flutter

tickling my soul

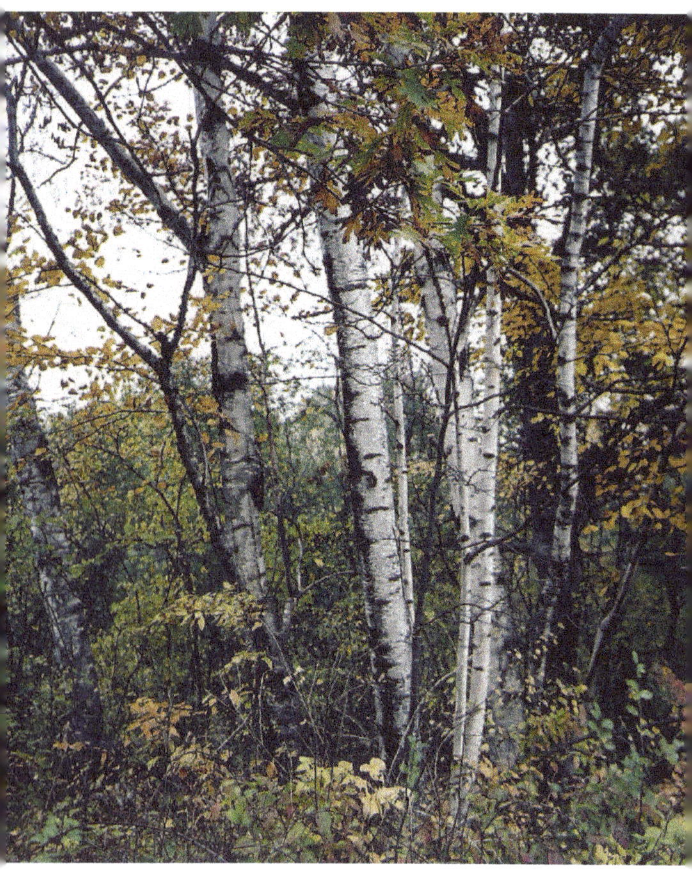

here in the woods

leprechaun peeks around trees

mischievous grin

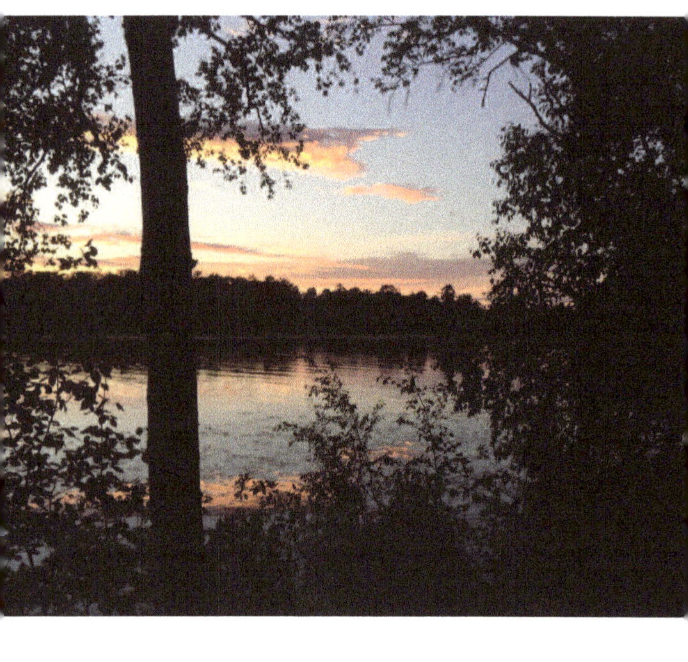

wistful yearning brings

remembrance of bygone days

a lifetime ago

www.ingramcontent.com/pod-product-compliance
Ingram Content Group UK Ltd.
Pitfield, Milton Keynes, MK11 3LW, UK
UKHW062253290726
14090UKWH00017B/658
9 780999 180112